GW00382268

Quotable Love

summersdale

QUOTABLE LOVE

Summersdale Publishers Ltd
46 West Street
Chichester
West Sussex
PO19 1RP
UK

www.summersdale.com

Printed and bound by Tien Wah Press

ISBN: 1-84024-663-4

ISBN 13: 978-1-84024-663-6

Quotable Love

When two **people** love each other, they don't **look** at each other; they look in the **same** direction.

Ginger Rogers

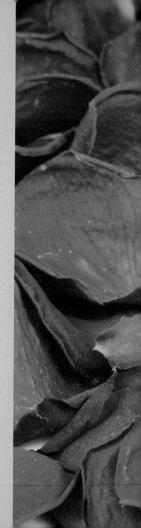

Life is a **flower** of which love is the **honey**.

Victor Hugo

There is **always** some **madness** in love. But there is also always some **reason** in madness.

Friedrich Nietzsche

I **love** you

Not **only** for what **you** are

But for what I am

When **I am** with you...

Roy Croft

A kiss is a **lovely trick** designed by nature to **stop speech** when words become superfluous.

Ingrid Bergman

Love is but the **discovery** of ourselves in others, and the **delight** in the **recognition**.

Alexander Smith

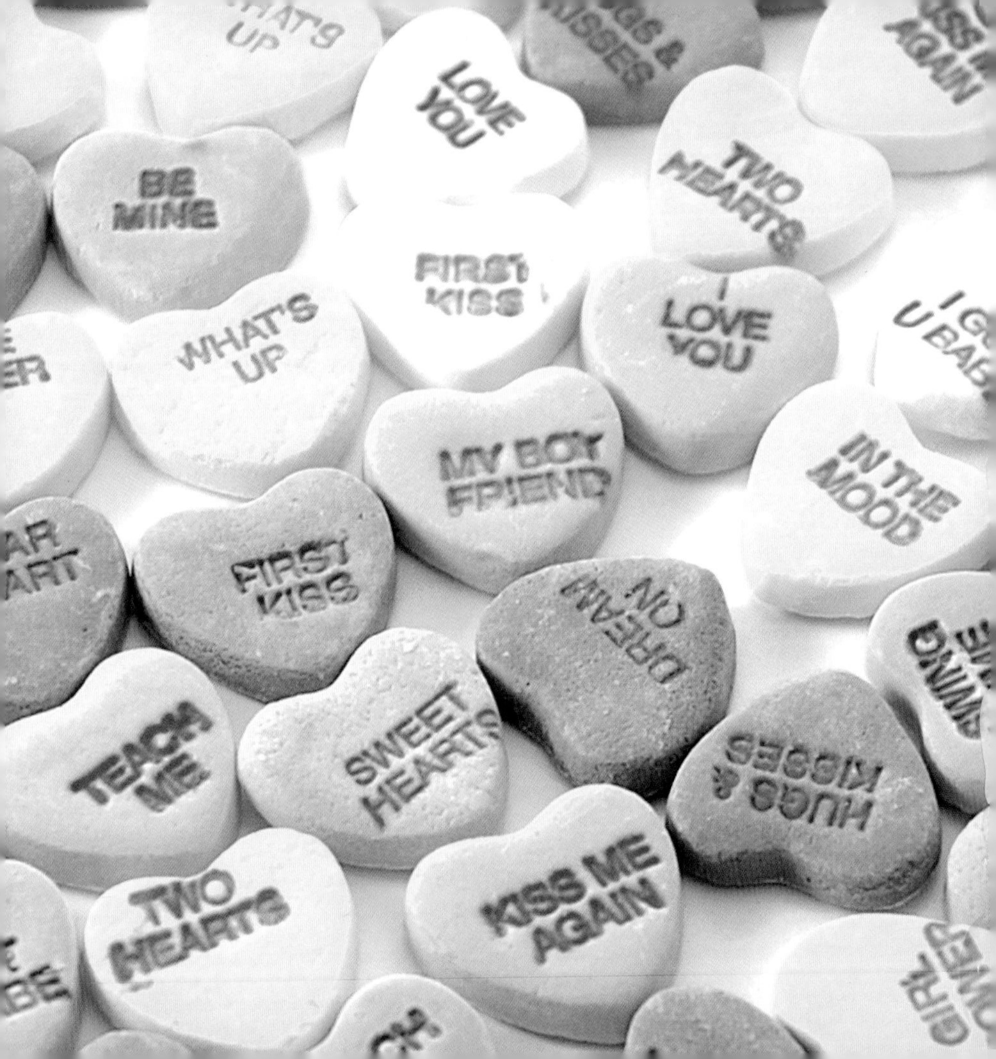
LOVE YOU
BE MINE
TWO HEARTS
FIRST KISS
WHAT'S UP
I LOVE YOU
MY BOY FRIEND
IN THE MOOD
FIRST KISS
DREAM ON
TEACH ME
SWEET HEARTS
HUGS & KISSES
KISS ME AGAIN
TWO HEARTS

There will always be **romance** in the world so long as there are **young hearts** in it.

Christian Nestell Bovee

Love at **first sight** is easy to understand; it's when two people have been **looking** at each other **for a lifetime** that it becomes a miracle.

Amy Bloom

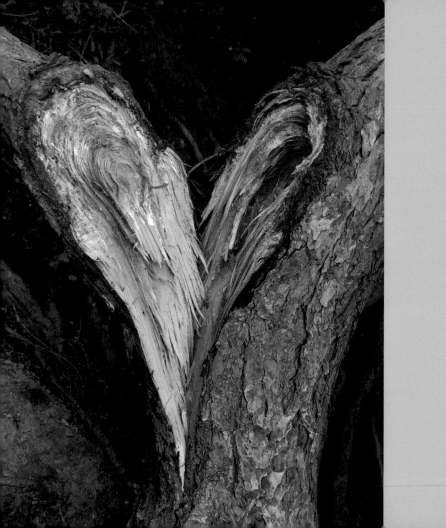

Love is a **canvas** furnished by **nature** and embroidered by **imagination**.

Voltaire

Love vanquishes time. To lovers, **a moment** can be eternity, **eternity** can be the tick of a clock.

Mary Parrish

If **grass can grow** through cement, love can find you at **every time** in your life.

Cher

To love and be loved is to **feel the sun** from **both sides**.

David Viscott

In love the **paradox** occurs that two beings **become one** and yet remain two.

Erich Fromm

Where **there is love**
there is no question.

Albert Einstein

We are, each of us, **angels** with only one wing; and we can only fly by **embracing one another**.

Luciano de Crescenzo

Anyone can be
passionate,
but it takes real
lovers to be **silly**.

Rose Franken

We **love** because it's the only true **adventure.**

Nikki Giovanni

Love one another and you will be **happy**. It's as **simple** and as **difficult** as that.

Michael Leunig

My bounty is as **boundless** as the sea,

My love as **deep**; the more I give to thee,

The more I have, for both are **infinite**.

William Shakespeare, *Romeo and Juliet*

Love is the **desire** to be irresistibly desired.

Robert Frost

A **kiss** makes the **heart** young again and **wipes out** the years.

Rupert Brooke

One who **walks** the road **with love**

will never walk the road alone.

C. T. Davis

Never **close your lips** to those whom you have **opened** your heart.

Charles Dickens

Love is like **smiling**; it **never** **fades** and is contagious.

Paula Dean

The anticipation of **touch** is one of the most potent **sensations** on earth.

Richard J. Finch

Love is **what you make it**

and who you make it with.

Mae West

Then seek not, **sweet**,

the 'If' and 'Why'

I love you now **until I die**.

Christopher Brennan

I love you. **I am at rest** with you. I have come **home**.

Dorothy L. Sayers

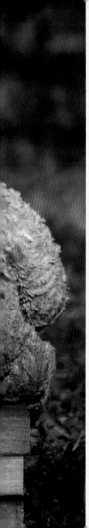

I want **love**, because love is the **best feeling** in the whole world.

Fairuza Balk

When we are **in love**

we seem to ourselves quite

different from what

we were before.

Blaise Pascal

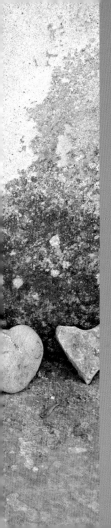

All **love is original**, no matter how many other **people** have loved before.

George Weinberg

Grow **old** along with me; the **best** is yet to be.

Robert Browning

If I know what **love** is, it is because of **you**.

Herman Hesse

You have to walk **carefully** in the **beginning** of love; the running across fields into your **lover's arms** can only come later when you're sure they won't **laugh** if you trip.

Jonathan Carroll

Two souls with but a **single** thought, **two hearts** that beat as one.

Friedrich Halm

You come to **love** not by finding the **perfect** person, but by **seeing** an imperfect person perfectly.

Sam Keen

Earth's the **right place** for love: I **don't know** where it's likely to go better.

Robert Frost

Lip on **lip**, and eye on eye,

Love to love, **we live**, we die;

No more thou, and no more I,

We, and **only we!**

Richard Monckton Milnes, Lord Houghton

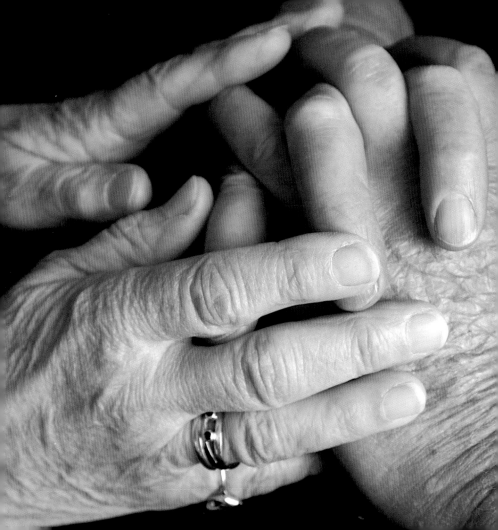

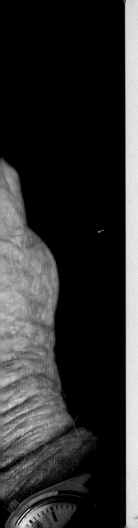

Once you **find love**, you find it. There isn't an **age** on love.

Candace Cameron

I can **summon** at will all my **happiest** hours,

And relive my past **buried** in your lap...

Charles Baudelaire

Love lives **beyond**

The tomb, **the earth**, which **fades**

like dew...

John Clare

Love is like **pi** –
natural, **irrational**
and very important.

Lisa Hoffman

When **I saw you** I fell in love. And **you smiled** because you knew.

Arrigo Boito

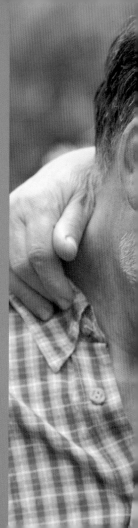

To **love deeply** in one direction makes us **more loving** in all others.

Madame Swetchine

Quotable Mothers

Milly Brown

Quotable Mothers

£5.99

ISBN 13: 978-1-84024-623-0

'Motherhood: all love begins and ends there.'
Robert Browning

Mum is most definitely the word in this charming collection of poignant quotations and beautiful photographs celebrating the most important women in our lives: our mothers.

Quotable Mothers is the perfect way to make any mum feel special. Whether for Mother's Day, a birthday or just to say thank you for all the great things they do, this book is the ideal gift for expectant mums, new mums and veteran mums to let them know just how special they are.

Quotable Animals

Milly Brown

Quotable Animals

£5.99

ISBN 13: 978-1-84024-598-1

'I am fond of pigs. Dogs look up to us. Cats look down on us. Pigs treat us as equals.'

Winston Churchill

Bursting at the seams with quotes and photos, this book is a delightful celebration of the world's favourite creatures.

From dogs to frogs this is a great gift for every animal lover.